# PIONEER
# SPECIES

❧

# PIONEER SPECIES

*poems*

❧

ROSS THURBER

GREEN WRITERS PRESS   *Brattleboro, Vermont*

Printed in the United States

10 9 8 7 6 5 4 3 2 1

Green Writers Press is a Vermont-based publisher whose mission is to spread a message of hope and renewal through the words and images we publish. Throughout, we will adhere to our commitment to preserving and protecting the natural resources of the earth. To that end, a percentage of our proceeds will be donated to environmental activist groups. Green Writers Press gratefully acknowledges support from individual donors, friends, and readers to help support the environment and our publishing initiative.

Green
writers
press

*Giving Voice to Writers Who Will Make the World a Better Place*
Green Writers Press | Brattleboro, Vermont
www.greenwriterspress.com

ISBN: 978-0-9994995-8-0

COVER ART BY ERIC AHO
WWW.ERICAHO.COM

for amanda

# CONTENTS

~

## GREEN POPPLEWOOD

## SUNBURNT JUNIPER

## STAG HORN SUMAC

## SNOW MELT, BLACK BROOK

# GREEN
# POPPLEWOOD

∼

# GROUND TRUTHED

Here is the long season of forgiveness.
Love leaves only the lilies
wanting from a ghostly harvest:
The fruit was too green to pick,
the stalks were torn from their roots.

Soon evening spring rains
will be the blessing and commission.
Skin will be night air.
Dawn throated songs begin
each day.

I am a poor king: bird on a branch,
stone picker, woodsman, herdsman.
My stables small, my fields flinty
pitched and far from the river.

My vestments made from the blotted
leaves of trout lily stitched
with lichen fast to the rock.

Sun skiff under a passing cloud
a ranging coronation of grace and speed:
Give up your grip, let down the floodgate.
The middling mountains will hold
your silt, wing flaps, meanders,
passing concerns.

# BELL FOUNDRY

Let winter sink into a soft spring night.
May valley fog rise to the foothills
and the foothills be buried in a purple cloak.

I'm giving up the torch for a bell.

One founded from river current,
sun stroked beech leaves
and April stippled light.

I'm giving up the torch for a bell.

A mold cast in ashes of rose,
heaving fieldstone, a frost seeded
tone that will reach all the bare places.

I'm giving up the torch for a bell.

A morning toll that makes the dew lapped
sounds of poems when you wake.

Here is the inverted vessel holding
no weighty burden
ringing with resonant airlessness,

peeling with the shape that makes
the sound of the fullness of time.

# HUNGER MONTH

The teeth of Artemis are made of milk and meat:
Rose apple tips sheathed in bud wood.
Virgins waiting for the swelling springtide.

Last season's grass is in the hay
in the corner of the loft:
a year moored briefly
in a green harbor.

March winds blow whitecaps
up river over islands
across empty meadows
into forest of collagen and resin.

Sinew is a ribbon of pang.
Morning moon flays a rack of trees.

Let's start with spring water,
drawn in the porcelain sink.
Scrub the silica, iron and salt,
brush earth from the skin.

Drink milk from the nipple
and eat meat from the thigh.

# MAKING SPRING

Milk and sugar
fill the cataract
with sweet blindness.
The brook pummels
stone on stone
your skin an eggshell
in an owl's nest.
Before we were animals
we were bird song,
cherry wood
smoke in the morning.
Abandon earth travel:
the clay before your feet
disappears into channels.
Drink a watercourse:
of honey maple lemon
and vinegar.

Little death, little death
press my lips: this sprig,
this bud from how began
what we have left.

# EASTER BLUES

The good news has yet to reach us
out here in the stale wood.

A low backs in from the shore,
stalling this heralded beginning
under a one hundred and twenty mile
damp shawl.
Poplar blooms spurt tattered lambs' fleece
strung out across the tree crowns.
A carcass left from a poor king's offering.

These remains are only scaffolding
around a ruined church:
Feathers on a reptile, a widow maker
chunked by woodpeckers.

We have suffered enough.

I climb the mountain to find a clearing.

Across the valley, the worsted
hills of New Hampshire are hung
indigo and wait to dry out.

I would like to start again
back at dawn. Look east.
Remember you are rising too,
and stop searching
for the living among the dead.

# IN MEMORIAM:
# EARLY MAY,
# COLD HOLLOW
# MOUNTAINS

Sun squints at the grave
hills with middling light
moving west to east
in the same manner
my ancient's milky eye
takes inventory of the field
in the valley
that after descending
from the mountain, splotched
with ramps and skunk cabbage,
land the home coming green.


Her skin was blotted like trout lily.
Eyes vaulted blue—Her hair, her white
tennis shoes the last remaining snow drifts.
Her impish gait still shuffling uphill
looking for the wild flowers.


Light pools blue in the hollows
and bruised on the ridges.
Eyelids shut with the warmth
and inner tissue of birch bark.

Lilies, trillium, violets
mark the open woods
and decorate the headstones.

# BURN PERMIT

After dusk is spun to a silver thread
stitched through a green evening song,
night shudders in like a horse cooling down.

After hierarchies and frameworks have saber-
rattled and clicked limb to limb
holding steady through early high winds,

roots blind and dumb hold fast to their secrets.
Bloodroot kindle the first flitting lights
across the grove, their white globes half full

with this morning's passing shower.
By how many graces till we know, for sure,
that deep breathing night is here to stay?

From the roof of a mouth of a wood frog
to the paper from the town that says
commence with your torching.

Free holding damp and hissing pile
of April offering
a smudge-pot island of hope and return.

# POOR MAN'S FERTILIZER

Exalted spring
and organs billow anthems

before daffodils lift high their yellow banners
in the plantings and discarded places.

And after trees can no longer live
by swollen bud alone,

a tom turkey ventures out unbidden
puffing his blue head like a beacon.

And the plowed fields have settled with the deep
nights behind them –

there is a late snowfall: as if winter needed to
succor its charges on the way out

like a lover making the bed
before leaving

as if to say: this is a final departure,
here this is snow with ardor:

Nitrogen, sulfur and water.

Soon you'll be so full of June light
You won't know what to do with yourself.

# KAIROS

I have watched closely, waiting for the poppies to shift
from their green nodding heads

the monochromatic husk to blow apart and shed
into two neat lime wedges

unfurling into a red rapturous dress
with the abandon no homeland

and no country will claim.

Last night's storm left the pistil wet,
the huddled orthodoxy of stamens bent,

black pollen filled the cracked lines of my hands
serving as my calendar and my work log.

In the gaping half risen morning
I know you're awake: breathing

to keep from drowning in a slipstream
of addled air. The musk of blackberry blossoms

lifts to the thunderhead, orchard grass pollen
sandblasts the gravestones in the cemetery.

I circle my finger around the bottom of the flower cup.
One working dial on a broken clock.

# EASTERTIDE

You can still see through the trees
if you look through the patch of hardwoods
the farmhouse shines like a white boulder
lodged between two old maples.
Close by is a maroon barn with a new blue
roof grafted like a hopeful scion.

Across the mowing,
two men pull brush to the walled edge.
The heavier oak pieces they brace
against their backs and pull.
The lighter black cherry limbs
they arrange in piles and carry in bundles.

They remark to one another
how much has changed when these trees
fell like shadows into the snowy field
and they worked just to keep their hands warm.

"This is the time of year when nature is in suspension,"
one said. "You're fooled nothing is happening."

"This is the season that cleanses your palate,"
said the other. "It seems that all you need
is work, water, and air."

Beyond the field, where the woods gathers to the edge
as if any shoreline is a marvel, as if this is where

The news will break:

A grove of Popple bends to do its washing.
The petals on the new flowers mottle
grey and wave in the light
breeze like white linen wrappings.

# PETAL DROP

The genius of spring
is amnesty from falling.

World on the rise,
funeral pyres by the river,
bonfires on the moor,
even gravity is losing
a foothold.

Spirits return to green
aching grass
and never even touch
the ground.

# SUNBURNT
# JUNIPER

~

# COLD JUNE RAIN

Why wait for the gloaming
or a still water dirge
when the pasture is here
and the brook runs swift
under a witch hazel.
Ferns breach the ground
by the fistful offering up
green and prehistoric bouquets.

Thoughts, any thoughts
streak with dace
upstream in a light
before there was a light.
My heart's completely covered
in moss—it bleats and nudges
like a nursing lamb.
My chest is a cavity
for nesting.

Our passage is waiting
in a black locust that fell
across the hay mowing,
moored by a single root
in the green lapping forage.

The blooming tree oars
across the field,
a dory full of white petals.
Its wake of honeyed air
settles into the valley.

# MOUNTAIN FASTNESS

Starts with an intercession for lake, meadow and wood,
a clearing and then a path between the pointed
spruce and the flat needled fir lit at dusk
like a votive offering its anointed air.
I crush their tips for memory.


The ritual moss underfoot,
you stop to admire a glacial boulder calved by the trail
and a lichen's life's work comes off as feathered
stone dust with the brush of your hand.
Quiet is the mountain inside and out.
The greenstone serpentinite
long since froze its fires.


At the summit, more of a field than a peak,
more openings than closures:
the din of the kingdom settles below.


We came here to watch the moon
but it sank before it could rise
on a spoon of melted cream,
on your ginger lips,
your mouth, God
made small so that your heart
rises only so high as your throat.

# THE COWS ARE WALKING
# THROUGH THE FOREST

In a ribbon of milk and pasturage
carried with sweet sacred habit,

they keep to the dry hummocks above
the spring seeps, reaching for mouthfuls

of raspberry leaves and witch hazel
before arriving at the clearing.

Morning fog rises and rises wraithlike,
making new hills, new mountain ridges

that burn off, leaving this old arable
hoof-worn hill drenched with dew.

The cows are walking through
the forest leaving a trail of crushed

needles before entering the maw
of a heavy summer day.

# DAY LABOR

Every dawn the longing rises a bit
settles, seeks succor and becomes a prayer.

Middle day slips on like a fly mask
over my pastured head.
Torpor stands patiently in the shrill shade.

I imagine there must be something that won't break
won't fester,  needs no help to aid its motion.
Goes on forever.

Evening blessed evening save for me
your ultramarine.

# PIVOT

The wild rose is aloft now,
Song of Solomon airborne
citrus-scented blossoms on the wing.

Shimmering bridal light
and a green wave ripple the fields.

The calf born in high grass will know its not wild:

  the crippled led to the shore,
  the blind offered sweet fruit,
  the dumb speak with the flute of a veery,
  the deaf hear approaching horses in the night.

Your dispirited husk shucked to the wayside.

The lake is quiet but is looking back
at you with the reflection of mercury.

# BLUE NOTES

The grass is spellbound under a golden horn
with an ensemble that beachheads and slips into a groove.

Windrows tedded at noon, raked and woven at two
baled around three o'clock.

The player's throat is dry, air cured
with each green blade buzzing

when summer enters the room.

The fuel pump on the tractor chortles diesel,
the cable on the baler splinters,

the valve stem on the wheel is shot,
studs loosen from their rim; the hub cracks a high treble.

Evening follows the rhythm section and trickles in.

Bruised light is sweet on the metal,
shadows reach across the field and meet.

Dew in her club dress will make rust float in a droplet.

A fox with one sable leg arrives at dusk, cases the meadow,
stays until closing time.

# WHEN STORMS CAME
# IN THE LATE AFTERNOON

We all knew they were coming.
I called to the cows through the patch
of pines above the east pasture
where earlier they fanned out grazing.

I called but they would not budge.
Air heavy, turning green and melancholy
choked with goldenrod and Queen Anne's lace.

The meadow slope full of fallen halos.

What could these angels bring
that we don't have now?

When I arrive, the cows look
through me in silent unison
waiting, perhaps, for something more.

Thunderheads way up on the hill
have already disbanded the lake,
raked the mountain—approaching
the valley with the heavy scent
of mint and lightning.

It's enough for one to start:
A collective reluctant rising begins
like the end of a prayer, each one
with her own accord and manner.

I follow.
My love is a disappearing form
melting into the edge of the wood.

# FOR MRS. PUTNAM

You begin as a grass matted stream
in the morning coursing through a heavy
field with mint, boneset and Joe Pye weed.

You fool me with slow burning fog
and mountain springs giving
away their source.

You move along with the shudder
and vibration of a roller chain
missing the teeth on the sprocket.

You reside in the old woman:
her house dress stained with blotches
of red raspberries that she picks alone
in the entanglement around her papered shack.

# WHAT NOW?

Sometimes the moon is a plum line
centered just over the field, still
only for a quick reading.

And then, sometimes, it's like a trout,
a mottled flash quivering through the trees
in and out of sight,
spawning from one end of the north woods
to the other.

Other times, the moon is a peach, pricked
by a pointed fir before clearing the horizon.
It peels and drizzles a sugar cape
of dew across the canopy and into the ferns,

leaving for us the only record:
The pit of a stone fruit
under the hinge of a collapsed threshold
that remains as cool as dirt.

# AUBADE

The watchman stumbles across the field
with a broken limb of sumac—torch snuffed out.
Lovers in the woods are well-warned
morning is a mute swan.

First glance of light falls from your temples
to the dimple in your shoulder
that holds the lyric
like a parting glass.

# STAG HORN
# SUMAC

❧

# BOUQUET

Pear blush and cedar bough
borders grove ferns dripping

Whitman—frond water
from drunken ledges.

Plath in the river valley
Burns off by ten.

Antler velvet, crow feather.

Broken eggshell sky
in the morning.

India ink filling in
the little wood by night.

# ECLIPSE

*While yet on earth*
*To be like the creator even in shadow*
*Is to be blessed in the foretaste.*

Bach Cantata #39

It must be something in the linkage yoking
the space in the periphery. An unerring
light that purls through the undercarriage,
beads off the coats of animals never moving
from their warm thicket beds in the woods.

The lunar eclipse began unceremoniously
while rain pelted the slate roof.
My rising more from instinct and duty
than to witness. My knowledge
only a pixelated, half-assed appreciation
of celestial courses.

But I saw it
unwittingly from the milk house porch:
Rain still spitting, clouds breaking in the west,
the penumbra falling from the upper left hand
corner as if some angel had read this heavenly body
before—marking the page, folding it between her fingertips
knowing I may be here to read it.

# NOVEMBER IS A MIDDLE DISTANCE

In the suppleness of these lasting days
is a milk-sun lodged in the throat.
The doe-eyed wood looks back
like a startled bride at her groom:
foreign, hale and in fighting trim.
Winged seed jewels lay at her bedside.
Her summer gown pooled at her feet.

There is a new edginess now
caving stone walls making
rusted barbed wire slack.
A rifle shot? No, a dump truck,
tailgate ringing in the valley.
The falling hammer's metal upon metal.
The silver piston eases the bed down.

The stakes are higher and unrepeatable.
Hook rubs from antlers shred bark
down to the bare stem.
Hoof scrapes yield territories
of musk and piss.

Stay quick and silver hemmed
through this ineffable descent.
You are a coddled seed buried
in the womb, a fire to tend to
between empty volleys,
missed trajectories and months
and months of echoing loneliness.

# WILLOUGHBY GAP, OCTOBER

Blushing hills are melting
wood and nectar.
The last breaths are water-rippled,
blurred histories.
Evergreens, the stoic pallbearers,
don't even flinch in the rush of dusk
when evening tremors in
like a funeral train.

# SNOW MELT,
# BLACK BROOK

∿

# SMOKE de AMBERGRIS

We have come to this field for years now
to take stock of this humble outlook:
snow, matted grass, loam, bedrock.

Blue moon in a gossamer gown,
snow falls into the smallest places:
on the burnt pistils of goldenrod
 into the silver dorsal valleys of spruce
needles. With the weight of diamonds,
the whole bough bends bejeweled and filigreed.

If this night be the measure of time,
then let me take the right hand
and then the left hand and hold
them still.

If I brought you here then you took me there
to discover the ilk of beauty that left me
dumbfounded:

First it was the women of the Parthenon
shrouded in black floating out of their white columns.

And then the Singer Sargent painting,
a woman taking in the suitors from a perfume
scented with perfectly coiled rope, blood-stained hands
and eyes fixed on the horizon.

Tonight we firmly witness together the mountain
bowing her head
to slip on the chain that holds the moon like a glowing
stone close to the breast of this hillside.

# UNDER RUGGED STARS

Under rugged stars and silken snows,
mine is a love that can be fire-bricked,
pried and leveled over.
A winter-shed soldered with blue.
Deep river valleys welded with ice.

May I trace the circle where
the color of your skin changes
to mercury in the west.

Each night is an aria of stalking
hunger, hemlock bough springing
its weight under a sinking morning moon.

# SAVE FOR SNOW BUNTINGS

Hide-bound from head to toe,
I am pinched and stone cold,
a landmass with a raw interior.

I kneel on milk house concrete
and wait for the first blast of cindered
air from the salamander heater.

Suffering must come from the facsimile
we make for our poor adaptation.
Up—armored but naked.

According to the directions on the heater:
It runs on kerosene, diesel,
home heating and two types of jet fuel.

Maybe this is praying for tenderness:
going back to the blown field, being
ripped under the curl of a squall.

And memory: for nothing:
a flock of birds, a dervish plume
turned on a polar headwind.

# OXBOW

Come, come now, come up.

A meander will only go so far as a crescent,
the current having plied away the loess
and loosened the sandy loam
making way through the roots leaving skeletal
remains and returning to a straighter channel.

A bed of stones and cinnamon ferns
keep the memory the way a beeswax
candle holds a flame when light
has left the bottom of winter.

Come, come now, come up.

Two grouse light from afternoon feeding,
making a low arc under the bottom
branches in a short calculated flight.

The cattle are in from the mowings and lie
under the barn: eating, breathing, making
just enough heat to keep the frost
out of the dry-laid foundation.

The lake ice is harder now than last month
when a young man took his team of oxen
across one of the northern lakes hoping
to get a jump on the logging season.

The skim of ice was clear over the inland fjord
but had as much strength as the sun and let go

sinking the young roan-yolked team,
eyes clear, pressing and fixed ahead.
The ash bows firm to their wet coats
the boy behind gently
as he had been before, calling.

Come, come now, come up.

# FELLING

Undoing creation is work.
It is aiming the notch-cut making a hinge,
plunging until the saw spins teeth
that cut nothing, every last fiber
severed leading to that moment:

chainsaw throttles down to an idle
the heft sundered, the longing severed,
knowing when the green bough
weighted with snow is sun-found
released and summoned.

He offers the crown to the roots
in a bright winter ground vestment
littered with whorls of needles.
Light pines for an empty space.

The woodsman leaves the forest
with a certain kind of hunger.

# INTERVAL

The sun washes over calves lying in a pod
in a pen, heads on necks and shoulders
and backs, new pine sawdust
smells like vanilla, night ice holds on past noon,
red shadows on the snow deep in the ravine.
By four o'clock I know the sap will not run today.

Divinity shelters under a hemlock
in the bright, slow-falling snow.
Air brings a thaw of bergamot
steeped in the tannins of roots.

# WINTER MERMAIDS

Shadows flare like fetlocks from trees
across the rucked snowfield.
Morning comes here first to the high coves
and saddles above the village and sputtering
river sunk in the cold below.

The tops of yesterday's felling splayed
across the edge of the field are scrolled
with deer tracks: They fed in the dark
on the meaty buds.

The wood cutter is working early
with clarity and purpose.
His pouch of tools—scrench, and saw file
and wool coat hang on a beech limb in the early
morning sun above the snow drifts.

High winter continuum: one ice crystal staked
upon another and another.

The deer, the wood, the man, the longed-for purification.
The hope, the work, thrown off by

last nights dream of winter-mermaids
plunging under the snow
the liquefaction of their hair, their honed
bright black eyes

leaving a slipstream
as they dove for pearls.

# Animal Husbandry

Every day they lick
the salt block just out of reach.
My job: put it back.

# HYGGE

While snow fills the grove
orchid blooms above the sink.
Come, burrow in.

# SAGITTARIAN VALENTINE

Two anchoring lights moor
the voluminous black lake.
A ghost star veers across
the quick ice
while a frozen Carillon rings
the hours in a constellation
of air spaces singing
from lapped bell chambers.
Tonight in the monastery,
along the northern headlands,
the brothers have sung
and prayed, Compline received.
In the orchards along the shore,
still studded with vermillion fruit,
the moon will rise,
light the nave, the narthex
the last waking thought.
Maroon me, November,
yield with grace,
all these wishes when you find
them in your sun-drenched
elasticity of May.

# WINTERING GROUNDS

In a cold spell, when it gets down below zero for night

after night, the farm loses its marvel and looks for a mechanic
to cobble, cope and help maintain fluidity. That is why I

lie in bed on one of those nights and run down my pre-flight
check down before I sleep:

Is the water drained and valve closed in the calf barn?
Are the doors shut and fastened in the cow barn?

Is the milk house latched and secure?
Are the tractor engine heaters plugged in?

Morning arrives vacant, the remnant of a star.
It's too cold for much else besides verification. So I make my
    rounds.

Across the small field by the barn, a blue TV screen flickers
    like a pilot light
in my neighbors' dark house—and heats the empty room.

Further up the road, a warm lamp light glows in my sister's
    house.
Baby Delia's up before dawn with her mom to nurse.

I prepare the cows for their morning routine; they stretch
   in their sawdust beds
their noses and whiskers frosted like frozen marsh grass.

I am always startled when I walk to unplug the cord from
   the block heater on the tractor
and four English Sparrows perched on the fuel lines
   quickly, trance-like, take flight.

# MOUNTAINS FADING
# INTO THE NEW YEAR

The winter stream bed is swollen and enameled
all at once, and the husks of angels have left me
soaked, tired and overjoyed.
I wrap my hands around a warm thermos
and imagine what mystery could make
you such a vessel:


holding your rising and falling,
your surprising weather, your heady arrivals
and spectral disappearances:
Just like mountains fading into a new year.

~

# ACKNOWLEDGEMENTS

❦

I am grateful to the editors of the following magazines where these poems first appeared.

*Blood Root Literary*: "Bouquet", "Blue Notes"

*Vermont Life:* "Cold June Rain"

I am grateful for the catalyst, support and inspiration of: Dede Cummings, James Crews, Melany Kahn, Suzanne Kingsbury, Robert Lawson, Emily Mason, Lisa Mendelsund, Julia Shipley and the Tuesday night Salonista's—where it's always spring.

*Pioneer Species* was typeset in Bembo which is a typefact that goes back to one of the most famous printers of the Renaissance, Aldus Manutius. In 1496 he used a new weight of a roman face, formed by Francesco Griffo da Bologna, to print the short piece 'De Aetna' by Pietro Bembo. This very typeface would eventually be of such importance that the development of print typefaces is unthinkable without it.

The first developmental phase was defined by the influence of the classic Roman forms, indentifiable by the slight slant of the lower case s and the high crossbar of the lower case e, which in time took on less and less of a slant. The Monotype Corporation in London used this roman face as the model for a 1929 project of Stanley Morison which resulted in a font called Bembo. Morison made a number of changes to the 15th century forms. He modified the capital G and instead of the italic which Manutius originally had in mind, he used that from a sample book written in 1524 by Giovanni Tagliente in Venice. Italic capitals came from the roman forms.

❧

DESIGN BY DEDE CUMMINGS
BRATTLEBORO, VERMONT